THE
GREATEST
CATHOLIC
PRESIDENT

THE GREATEST CATHOLIC PRESIDENT

GARCIA MORENO OF ECUADOR
1821-1875

Frank M. Rega, S.F.O.

ANGELUS PRESS
2915 FOREST AVENUE
KANSAS CITY, MISSOURI 64109

Published in the British international Catholic monthly, *Christian Order*, in the May and June-July 2008 issues.

Library of Congress Cataloging-in-Publication Data

Rega, Frank M.
  The greatest Catholic president : Garcia Moreno of Ecuador 1821-1875 / Frank M. Rega.
    p. cm.
  Includes bibliographical references.
  ISBN 978-1-892331-69-4
  1. García Moreno, Gabriel, 1821-1875. 2. Presidents--Ecuador--Biography. 3. Ecuador--Politics and government--1830-1895. 4. Ecuador--History--1830-1895. 5. Catholics--Ecuador--Biography. I. Title.
  F3736.G3R44 2009
  986.6'06092--dc22
  [B]
                              2009012098

©2009 Frank M. Rega
All rights reserved. No part of this book may be reproduced or transmitted in any form or by any means, electronic or mechanical, including photocopying, recording, or by any information storage and retrieval systems without permission in writing from the publisher except by a reviewer who may quote brief passages in a review.

ANGELUS PRESS
2915 FOREST AVENUE
KANSAS CITY, MISSOURI 64109
PHONE (816) 753-3150
FAX (816) 753-3557
ORDER LINE 1-800-966-7337
www.angeluspress.org

ISBN 978-1-892331-69-4
FIRST PRINTING—April 2009

Printed in the United States of America

Contents

The Greatest Catholic President 1

His Character 7

His First Term: 1861-1865 9

The Concordat with Rome 11

Interim Years 15

The Saviour of Ibarra 19

The Second Term: 1869-1875 23

The Social Program 29

Consecration of the Nation
  to the Sacred Heart of Jesus 33

Notes 39

Bibliography 41

The Greatest Catholic President

Few Catholics today know the story of Gabriel Garcia Moreno. This devout and holy man, blessed with a keen intellect and noble character, briefly re-established the shining light of Christendom in a small corner of the New World during the nineteenth century. His contemporary, one Charles Darwin, had been at work in some islands in that same area of the globe, known as Ecuador, developing his false theory of species evolution that would become the philosophical bulwark of the godless societies of the future. In the meantime in the Old World, another contemporary, Blessed Pope Pius IX, was suffering through the forced seizure of the Papal territories, during the creation of a unified Italy.

Garcia Moreno's role in Catholic history is so significant that the Blessed Virgin Mary foretold his coming more than two centuries before his 1821 birth. During the Church-approved apparitions of Our Lady of Good Success, an unusually specific prophecy was given to a holy Conceptionist nun in Quito, Ecuador, on January 16, 1599. On that date, Our Lady revealed to Venerable Mother Mariana de Jesus Torres details of the life of a future president of the Republic of Ecuador–a country which did not even exist at the time. Our Lady of Good Success, whom the Archdiocese with the permission of Rome would crown Queen of Quito, spoke the following oracle:

> In the nineteenth century a truly Christian president will come, a man of character whom God our Lord will give the palm of martyrdom on the square adjoining this Convent of mine. He will consecrate the Republic to the Sacred Heart of my Most Holy Son, and this consecration will sustain the Catholic Religion in the years that will follow, which will be ill-fated ones for the Church. These years, during which the accursed sect of Masonry will take control of the civil government, will see a cruel persecution of all religious communities, and it will also strike out violently against this one of mine.[1]

One of the smallest South American countries, Ecuador became an independent and sovereign republic on May 18, 1830. Previously, it had been part of "Gran Columbia" after Simon Bolivar liberated that territory from Spain in 1819. Secessionist movements soon followed, resulting in the establishment of the breakaway countries of Ecuador and Venezuela in 1830.

The Roman Catholic background of the newly independent Ecuador was reflected in its first constitution, which proclaimed that "The religion of the State is Catholic, Apostolic, Roman."[2] The government claimed the right of patronage, or *patronato*, a prerogative inherited from the Spanish colonial era. *Patronato* gave the State the power to unilaterally appoint church officials and bishops. Initially, this practice was not inimical to Church interests during the period when the Spanish colonies were ruled by loyal Catholics, but it became detrimental during the later eras of anti-clerical rule.

For the first fifteen years of its existence, Ecuador's politics and government were dominated by the figures of Vincente Rocafuerte and General Juan Jose Flores. Flores was president intermittently on four separate occasions for much of that period. He ruled with an iron hand, operating out of the nation's capital of Quito, located in the central highlands.

The highlands, or Sierra, consist of a great plateau lying between two parallel north-south chains of the Andes Mountains. The Sierra encompasses the mid-section of the country and is politically the most aristocratic and conservative. Though located near the equator, its elevation gives the highlands a spring-like climate most of the year. The fertile coastal areas to the west, and the under-developed Amazon basin to the east, the Oriente, comprise the other two segments of the nation. The main city of the liberal, mercantile coastal region is the important port of Guayaquil. The Galapagos archipelago, made famous by Darwin, also belongs to Ecuador.

In 1845, a youthful and relatively unknown writer, intellectual and lawyer by the name of Gabriel Garcia Moreno allied himself with a coterie of revolutionaries concerned about the increased dictatorial powers wielded by General Flores. This group, which included Rocafuerte, successfully overthrew the Flores administration and forced the disgraced president into exile. However, the half-dozen rulers who followed Flores were weak leaders, and the country descended into chaos. During this time Moreno's influence, power, and reputation for uprightness steadily increased–along with his ability as a civilian leader in armed conflicts. By 1859, when the last of the autocrats who had succeeded Flores was deposed, it was Moreno who headed a provisional three-man Junta that took temporary control of the reins of government in order to put down an armed rebellion. He was then only thirty-seven years old.

The final battle, which saw the Moreno-led triumvirate win control of the port city of Guayaquil from the rebels, took place on September 24, 1860. This was the feast of Our Lady of Mercy, also known as Our Lady of Ransom. Recognizing that the victory was owed to God, Moreno proposed that the army of the Republic should henceforth be placed "under the special protection of Our Lady of Ransom, and that every year on this great anniversary the Government and army should assist officially at the services of the Church."[3]

At the beginning of the next year, the provisional leaders resigned their commission, ceding their power to the nation's parliamentary Assembly. Garcia Moreno was subsequently appointed interim President until the electors could meet. The Assembly also accepted his proposal, and even went further by declaring Our Lady of Ransom the Patroness of Ecuador.

This has been only the briefest outline of a complex series of intrigues, skirmishes, civil wars, *coup d'états*, and overall instability that characterized Ecuador's early history, and which led to Moreno's formal election to his first term as president of the nation in 1861. In fact it was this very instability and confusion that led the populace to support the one and only man considered capable of ending the turmoil and uniting the nation.

During these formative years, both for the republic and for the man, Moreno had became convinced that the Catholic Religion was the only sure foundation for the growth and progress of the nation as well as for himself. He had undergone many personal trials and persecutions, including exile to foreign lands, which forged and strengthened his character and re-affirmed his faith in Christ.

An incident while he had been an exile in France was instrumental in his spiritual formation. As a youth Moreno had once considered entering the priesthood, and had even received Minor Orders. However, at the age of twenty he decided instead to pursue a degree in law, which he completed in only three years. He remained loyal to the Faith, although his interest and involvement with Catholicism was on an intellectual rather than a practical level. One day, while strolling with some of his companions in Paris, the conversation turned to religion and to the Church. His friends, who were secularists and atheists, began to attack Catholicism. Moreno took up its defense, and effectively countered their objections and arguments.

Exasperated, one of the group challenged Moreno's personal commitment to the Faith he was so forcefully defending. "When did you last go to Confession?" he disdainfully asked the Ecuadorian. Moreno bowed his head, acknowledging the truth behind the insinuation. The sudden realization that he had become lukewarm in the practice of his religion invoked deep compunction, and his former love for God and Christ was aroused anew. The inner conversion was immediate, and he replied to his companion, "You have answered me by a personal argument which may appear to you excellent today, but which will, I give you my word of honour, be worthless tomorrow."[4]

That very evening, after falling on his knees at home in prayer, penance, and self-reflection, he went out, found a priest, and made his confession. The next morning he received his Lord in the Holy Eucharist. From then on, daily Mass and prayer, especially the Rosary, became a life-long commitment. He had put his hand to the plough and never looked back. It was literally an overnight transformation, changing him from a lukewarm into a fervent Catholic.

Moreno spent much of the remainder of his Parisian exile engrossed in spiritual reading and study. He plunged into the twenty-nine volumes of *Histoire Universelle de l'Eglise Catholique* by the Fr. Rohrbacher, reading the entire opus an incredible three times over. Studying this work gave him an understanding of the nature of the relationship between the Church and the State that had been the foundation of Christendom–a relationship which respected the unique rights and privileges of the Church as the official religion and moral compass of the State. The laws and conduct of the secular government must be compliant with the Gospel of Christ, meaning that the State is in essence subordinate to the Church.[5]

HIS CHARACTER

Two episodes that reflected his firm and yet compassionate character occurred during the last phases of the civil war that had been won under the Moreno-led triumvirate. Some of the troops of the Provisional Government had been bribed by the opposition to renounce their loyalty to the administration. One evening they surrounded a building that was housing Moreno, and took him prisoner. They demanded under threats that he resign his position with the government. Moreno refused as a matter of principle, and for this stance he was to be executed on the morrow by the rebels.

On what was to be the last night of his life, he commended his soul unto God. However, being a man of action as well as prayer, he began to remonstrate with the lone guard assigned to him, in order to make him understand that this offence against an official of the government of Ecuador was treasonous. Moreno succeeded in arousing the man's remorse, and the guard fell to his knees, begging forgiveness. He then freed Garcia Moreno on the spot. The leader made his escape, stealing past the rest of the rebels, who were asleep in a drunken stupor after a night of pillaging and revels.

Then, after a few short hours, Moreno returned with a band of loyal troops and rounded up the insurgents, who were taken completely by surprise. Several of their ringleaders were arrested and condemned to death for treason by a council of war convened on the spot. Moreno gave them time to prepare for death and sent for a priest. One of the men was spared after evidence was presented that he was innocent, but the rest suffered the consequences of their acts.[6]

It was this type of firm but just action that caused his enemies, and some historians, to paint a picture of Garcia Moreno as a cruel and ruthless tyrant and dictator. But these rebels had been found guilty of desertion and treason against the State during a time of war, and any weakness on Moreno's part would have sent the wrong signal to any other insurrectionists. Furthermore, he only had the leaders executed, while the rank and file of the rebellious soldiers were not only pardoned, but allowed to rejoin their lawful commanders. A tyrant would not have acted in this way.

The second episode occurred as a prelude to the final battle at Guayaquil that brought victory to the Provisional Government in the civil war. The city of Guayaquil and much of the coastlands were in opposition hands, under the control of General Guillermo Franco. In an attempt to avoid further bloodshed of his countrymen on either side of the conflict, Garcia Moreno composed an admirable epistle to Franco, proposing that both he and Franco resign their respective commissions. The two leaders would retire into temporary exile, while the rest of Ecuador, both the coast and the interior, would submit to the authority of the Provisional Government based in Quito. In this way the disastrous civil war would be ended. The two men would return after stability had been established. Unfortunately, Franco refused this generous and noble proposal, going so far as to imprison the messenger who had carried the letter to him.

Following this setback, Moreno next had recourse to the Diplomatic Corps, composed of those foreign dignitaries and ministries stationed in Ecuador at the behest of their countries. Their pleadings also failed to move Franco, who wanted war and not peace. In the end this attitude was his undoing, and after a humiliating defeat at the hands of Moreno and his patriots at Guayaquil, Franco was forced to flee to Peru.[7]

This willingness of Moreno to step down from his leadership role in the Provisional Government for the good of the nation was followed by similar self-effacing gestures in subsequent years. Yet, his leftist detractors and opponents continued to paint him as a man of ruthless ambition–a dictator and a despot–a betrayer of his nation who deserved assassination. However, it was actually his deep-rooted Catholicism and his effort to establish Ecuador as a Catholic Republic that was the underlying reason for the leftist and Masonic opposition to his regime.

HIS FIRST TERM: 1861-1865

It was after the defeat of General Franco, on January 10, 1861, that Garcia Moreno and the other two Provisional leaders resigned their powers. In short order, the freely elected National Congress chose Moreno as President. This was the culmination and reward for his personal fifteen-year struggle combating the corrupt rulers who had exploited Ecuador ever since it had shed the yoke of Spain's monarchial rule. Initially he refused the honor, but yielded to the pleadings of his friends. The pie was sweetened when the legislature guaranteed him the power to unilaterally negotiate a Concordat with Rome, without the necessity for congressional ratification. The assembly also granted favorable treatment to a number of projects close to Moreno's heart: reform in the areas of education, finance, and the army, and also the creation of a modern system of transportation.

During the deliberations for an updated constitution, he persuaded the legislature to resist the strong influence of the liberals, who were threatening to put an end to the traditional union between Church and State in Ecuador. Thus, the revised constitution continued to uphold the status of Holy Roman Catholic Church as the official religion of the nation.

Decades of misrule had led to financial chaos, an undisciplined and dissolute army, and a government bureaucracy riddled with incompetent and corrupt political appointees. Moreno acted with unyielding firmness and determination to tackle these many problems. He quickly reversed these negative trends by successfully moving Ecuador in the direction of fiscal responsibility, military discipline, and honest government.

He felt, however, that the most serious problem he faced was the educational system, which had become almost totally secularized under the previous Masonic-influenced anticlerical regimes. In contrast, he wished Ecuador to be a paragon of Christian civilization, and understood that the key to this regeneration was the moral education of youth. The progressivist governments had stricken all mention of God and Christian morality from the schools which had been originally established in the colonial period, under the aegis of Catholic Spain. Moreno realized that the quickest and most efficient way to steep the schools in the teaching of the Christian religion was to introduce missionaries and Catholic educators from Europe. He thus began an extensive and successful effort to recruit foreign religious and to reform the schools.

When Moreno first assumed the presidency, there were no major carriage roads in all of Ecuador. People and goods traveling between the seaports and the mountains of the interior, including the capital of Quito, were dependent on horseback and mules. When he proposed to build a carriage road over 150 miles in length from Guayaquil to Quito, crossing the lowland swamps and climbing the rugged slopes of the Andes, many considered it a folly. He overcame the resistance, doubts, and open opposition of his countrymen by his determination and genius, and transformed the grumblers into enthusiastic admirers. To accomplish the feat, he employed thousands of workmen, accompanied by a priest and doctor day and night. Ten years later, during his second term in April of 1873, the task was finally completed. Almost at the same time, four other major carriage roads linking the country from the north to the south, and from east to west, were also completed. The effect on commerce and agriculture was profound, since now goods and produce could efficiently reach the seaports, and from there to America and Europe. The income of the State also rose dramatically, doubling within a few years.[8]

THE CONCORDAT WITH ROME

However, the most momentous accomplishment of his first term as president was the signing of a Concordat between Ecuador and Rome. Towards the end of 1861, Moreno dispatched a "Minister Plenipotentiary" to the Holy See, with full powers to execute the Concordat with Pope Pius IX on the rights and responsibilities of the Catholic Church in Ecuador. In the words of the vintage *Catholic Encyclopedia*, "The purpose of a concordat is to terminate, or to avert, dissension between the Church and the civil powers." It is both a civil and ecclesiastical law binding upon both powers, regarding matters which concern both.[9]

After months of negotiations, the document was signed in the fall of 1862 in Rome, pending Moreno's final approval. Its essential elements were, first, to reaffirm the position of Catholicism as the only religion of the State, "...to the exclusion of all other forms of worship, and of all societies condemned by the church."[10] Secondly, all levels of education, from primary to university, are to be regulated by Catholic principles and morals. All books dealing with religious education as such must be approved by the Bishops.

The role of government would not be limited to simply being a protector of religion, but the State was "...obligated to employ all proper measures for the propagation of the faith and for the conversion of the people found in that territory, and favor the establishment of the missions."[11] The civil government must also do its part in preventing the introduction into education of writings contrary to right faith and morals.

In addition, the law of *patronato* was suspended, with the Church having full liberty in matters relating to the administration of dioceses, property, and convocation of synods. The government was not to interfere with or prevent the Catholics of Ecuador from communicating directly with the Holy See. Regarding any vacant bishopric, three candidates selected by the bishops would be presented to the nation's President, who had three months to choose among them, after which time the choice would fall on Rome.

While a young priest, the future Pope Pius had traveled to South America and was astonished at the vast geographical area of many of the dioceses, which seemed to him to be much too large to be administered effectively. Thus the Holy Father, on his own initiative, included in the Concordat the announcement of the creation of three new bishoprics for Ecuador, a number that within twenty years would increase to seven additional dioceses. In the words of the Pope to the Minister Plenipotentiary, "Your zealous President wishes to regenerate his country: tell him that to succeed, he must plant the Cross. Wherever a Cross is placed, people group around it...."[12]

There were many other clauses in the document, but these were its main provisions. Moreno's representative returned from Rome with the completed Concordat, in expectation of its formal ratification in Quito in the presence of a Papal representative. But then a most interesting and unexpected complication occurred.

Moreno refused to approve the agreement because provisions for the reform of the clergy were inadequate. He was fully aware of the laxity and often scandalous behavior of the clergy, both secular and religious, whose corruption was encouraged during the anti-clerical governments. Moreno had desired that a Pontifical Delegate be assigned to Ecuador, with full powers to effect the necessary reforms, and to order the secularization of priests unwilling to comply. The Concordat had included clauses for the re-establishment of ecclesiastical tribunals, but the President knew that without vigorous enforcement measures, efforts at reform would be useless.

Moreno therefore sent his Minister back to Rome. There the astonished Pope was informed that the President would not sign the Concordat, since he was convinced that without addressing the reform of the clergy, the document would be a dead letter. Pius IX had omitted the clauses related to this issue because he had felt that sending a pontifical Delegate with enforcement powers would be too harsh a measure. His Holiness instead had favored an approach of gentle persuasion. The Ecuadorian Minister explained to him that Moreno knew first-hand the seriousness of the clergy crisis in his country, and that if the Holy Father were fully aware of the circumstances, he would concur with the President's judgment. Impressed by Moreno's determination and commitment, and by his boldness in refusing to sign the Concordat without the additions, the Holy Father acceded to the request for clergy reform.

Consequently, on April 22, 1863, the Concordat between the Holy See and the Republic of Ecuador was officially promulgated throughout the nation. Following a Pontifical Mass at Quito, the President and the Papal Delegate signed the document amid great pomp and ceremony, including artillery salvos and the simultaneous hoisting of the flags of the Papacy and Ecuador.

In the famous 1889 biography of Moreno by Fr. Augustine Berthe we read: "By this act of Christian policy, an act without parallel in the history of modern nations, Garcia Moreno raised himself above all statesmen since the days of St. Louis." Fr. Berthe adds, "... he restored true liberty to his country by placing her once more under the government of God."[13]

During this time, the opposition was not idle. Radicals and secularists were actively spreading propaganda among the people that the Concordat was a disastrous violation of the rights of the State. Making full use of the activist press, they succeeded in having a majority of anti-Concordat liberal Catholics elected to the popular Assembly. For many weeks the leftists, some of whom were sworn enemies of Moreno, attacked the president and his treasured Concordat in Parliament.

Moreno was determined to have no part in a revocation of the agreement. In a speech to the Chambers defending the document, he concluded with, "If the majority of the House should censure the acts of my administration, I will immediately resign my powers, praying Divine Providence to replace me by a magistrate fortunate enough to ensure the repose and the future well-being of the Republic."[14]

But Divine Providence acted in an unexpected way to save the President and the Concordat. War was suddenly declared on Ecuador by its neighbor New Granada. The very men who had been deriding Garcia Moreno moments ago now turned to him in the hour of need, realizing that only his strong leadership could save the nation. Within a few months, the aggressors were repelled on the battlefield by government forces. During this time of danger, serious opposition to the Concordat had been conveniently withdrawn.

In defending the agreement, Moreno had opposed the will of the majority of the popularly elected members of the House. But, as his biographer astutely points out, "As President he considered that his duty was, not to obey the people, but to guide and direct them. The revolution tows the country into an abyss. The counter-revolution marches ahead of the people, by the light of the Church, to enlighten and to save them."[15]

Interim Years

Prevented by the Constitution from succeeding himself, Moreno's term in office was over in 1865 after four years of service. However, he did propose a successor whom he hoped would continue his policies and support the Concordat. In the election that spring, his candidate roundly trounced the choice of the liberals and radicals. Moreno had only a few months left in his term of office.

Believing they now had only to deal with a "lame duck" president, a band of revolutionaries and plotters seized Ecuador's only warship near the port of Guayaquil. After murdering the captain and crew, the insurrectionists proceeded to commandeer two more ships, and anchored a good distance from the main port. Moreno was more than 150 miles away in the Quito area when news reached him of the rebellion. He immediately undertook a forced march with only one aide-de-camp, and three days later arrived in Guayaquil in the middle of the night. At the mere mention of the name of Garcia Moreno by the messenger who reported his arrival, the conspirators who had stayed behind in the city fled in haste.

Overcoming a string of obstacles, Moreno was able to obtain an English vessel, which he outfitted with four large cannons. Steaming out of port, he engineered a brilliant rout of the three ships of the rebels. As his victorious gunboat was making its way back to Guayaquil, a trial was held on board, at which the leaders of the captured insurgents were tried and convicted as pirates. Their sentence was death, the customary fate of such criminals. After meeting with a priest and making their peace with God, over two dozen men were executed.

Later, in the city itself, a prominent citizen was summoned to appear before President Moreno. Papers had been discovered on board one of the rebel boats that implicated the man in the treasonous plot. He was a lawyer and understood the penalty for sedition, but did not deny writing the letters. Moreno had no choice but to condemn him. Even the president's own eighty-year-old mother begged her son to show clemency. His reply was, "My mother!...ask of me what you will, but not an act of weakness which would lose the country."[16] He knew that only a show of strength in the face of treason and armed rebellion would ensure the peace and security of the nation. Of course his detractors–the leftists, Masons, radicals and liberals–accused him of being nothing short of the most ruthless of despots.

Moreno's successor in the presidency, Jeronimo Carrion, assumed office in the fall of 1865. The Constitution prevented the outgoing president from leaving the country for one year, unless authorized by Congress. Moreno, seeking the freedom to travel freely, asked for the authorization. However, in what was in essence a great tribute to the man, Congress refused the permission. His presence in Ecuador was considered essential to the security of the nation, which faced ongoing dangers, both domestic and foreign. Who else would be able to confront the plotters from the left, or stand up to armed threats from neighboring nations? By an overwhelming majority, the Parliament voted that "...a man so necessary to the safety of the Republic" must be prohibited from leaving during the coming year.[17]

However, President Carrion proved unable to stand as firmly as did his predecessor against the machinations of the liberals. In order to appease them, he countermanded the order of Congress, and sent Moreno out of the country as minister to Chile, which was at war with Spain. Moreno's inveterate enemies saw this as a double blessing. First, the hated Catholic conservative would finally be out of the country, and secondly, it was an opportunity for the conspirators to arrange matters so that he would not return alive to Ecuador.

In the summer of 1866, Moreno set out from Guayaquil with a small entourage that included his eight-year-old niece. Numerous warnings had reached him that his life was in danger, but he resolved to place his trust in God. The first stop on the way to Chile was a diplomatic visit to Peru. The steamer from Guayaquil dropped them off at a port city. From there a train carried the party to Lima, where an official delegation was awaiting their arrival. At the station, Moreno was the second of the group to descend the platform, and he turned around to assist his young niece. At that instant, shots suddenly rang out, with two bullets fired at his head. Although wounded on the forehead, he spun around toward his assassin and grabbed his arm, just as the culprit discharged his revolver a third time. Had he cowered and fled instead of boldly turning on his assailant, the third shot might have been fatal, instead of being deflected. The police seized the shooter just at the moment that he was again aiming his pistol at Moreno's head.

Upon hearing of the incident, the president of Peru sent his personal carriage to bring Moreno to the Presidential Palace. In spite of this official commiseration, justice was not to be done. The assassination attempt had been ordered by the lodges. Unfortunately, the judges were also Freemasons, and they deliberately delayed the trial long enough for memories to fade and witnesses to disperse. Moreno later resumed his journey to Chile amid the disgraceful news that the would-be assassin had been acquitted. Such was the scope and power of the revolution.

On the other hand, his six-month diplomatic mission in Chile was an outstanding success, and he concluded a number of important treaties between that nation and Ecuador. Upon his arrival he had been hailed as a hero for his bravery under fire. Consequently, no one dared to violate his safety and well-being during his pleasant and fruitful stay in that country.

When he returned to Ecuador, he found the Carrion administration in a state of collapse following a complex chain of political intrigues and maneuvers. In order to avoid a takeover of the nation by the radicals, Moreno was besieged by the conservatives to engineer a rescue of the State. He quickly formed an alliance with his political friends and was able to convince Carrion to resign in favor of Javier Espinoza, a good Catholic who was esteemed by the people. Espinoza was to finish the remaining eighteen months of Carrion's term.

The Saviour of Ibarra

Once again Moreno's decisiveness had restored stability to the nation. However, by this time he had made up his mind to withdraw from public life and to retire to his hacienda in the north. After his first wife had passed away, he remarried a young bride, but they had recently mourned the death of their little girl. His intention now was to lead a quiet life at the hacienda with his devoted wife amid the quiet woods and meadows. He would make use of his extensive knowledge of agriculture to cultivate the land and tend his herds. Although not a rich man, here he could lead the life of a gentleman farmer–a *terrateniente*–surrounded by the bounty that nature had lavished on Ecuador. However, it would be the force of nature itself that would conspire with God to return him to the path marked out by his prophetic destiny.

Only a few short months after establishing himself at the hacienda, the urgent report reached him of a severe earthquake and volcanic eruption in the northern province of Imbabura. The upheavals, which lasted for four days in mid-August of 1868, had devastated the provincial capital, Ibarra. More than half of its ten thousand inhabitants were killed. Many of the survivors were seriously injured or still trapped in the rubble. But instead of being rescued, they were cruelly robbed and plundered by roving gangs of bandits and impoverished indigenous peoples, pouring out of the mountains. The government at Quito predictably turned to the one man who could effectively restore order out of this chaos, Gabriel Garcia Moreno. The retired patriot quickly accepted his appointment as civil and military governor of the entire province of Imbabura, and set off for Ibarra at once.

He divided the troops under his command into two parts–one to undertake a search and rescue in the rubble and succor the wounded, and the other to fight off the pillagers. He sent out an appeal for food and supplies, which began arriving from all of Ecuador, including his own hacienda. With the advent of the provisions, "price gouging" merchants also made their appearance. Moreno, with his usual firmness, dealt with these types by having them publicly flogged! It only took about a month for him to restore order and stability to the devastated area. A tent city was established for the survivors, who were already designing the plans for a rebuilt capital city. Upon his departure, Moreno was hailed by the people as "the saviour of Ibarra." In fact, the ladies of the area later presented him with a medal set in diamonds with that very inscription.

Although warmly congratulated by public officials of every stripe, behind his back the liberals and socialists continued their personal vendetta against him. Presidential elections were on the horizon, and the conservatives began a popular movement to draft him as their candidate. The response was overwhelming. Moreno, who had resumed his retirement at his hacienda, reluctantly accepted the nomination, but only after making clear the basics of his platform: "Respect and protection for the Catholic Church; firm adhesion to the Holy See; education based on faith and morals..."[18] Officials would be appointed according to their merits and ability, rebellions against order would be summarily suppressed, and peaceful relations would be maintained with allies.

In stark contrast to these noble aspirations, the opposition journals portrayed Moreno as "a tyrant, an assassin, a hypocrite, a violator of laws, and the executioner of honest men."[19] The radicals were not about to rely on the results of the upcoming elections, and began plotting the overthrow of the government of reigning President Espinoza. The conspirators had picked a date in January of 1869 to launch their revolt in the key cities of the nation. President Espinoza, as well as most of the citizenry, realized there was a conspiracy afoot. Unfortunately, Espinoza was too weak and vacillating to take the necessary steps to stop the rebellion. In order to prevent the violent overthrow of the republic, Moreno's friends and supporters converged on his hacienda. They implored him to return with them to Quito to lead the effort to suppress the impending insurrection.

After careful deliberation, the would-be gentleman farmer agreed. In a series of daring maneuvers he quickly took personal control of the army at Quito. In the meantime the leading citizens and government officials formally deposed Espinoza, and declared Moreno the Acting President. They also planned to convene a national convention to revise the constitution. Moreno accepted the interim presidency on the condition that, "once order is restored and the Constitution reformed, I will resign my powers....Even if I were again elected, I should refuse the presidency."[20]

After a series of forced marches, he unexpectedly appeared with his troops at the liberal hotbed of Guayaquil, and prevented the planned uprising by immediately placing the entire province under a state of siege. In short order other cities renounced the progressives and swore their loyalty to the Acting President. As a result, the rule of law was affirmed in the entire nation, and the leaders of this latest conspiracy were either exiled or tried by military tribunal.

Garcia Moreno had saved the nation from civil war without a single shot being fired! He had accomplished this victory by the sheer force of his genius, charismatic leadership and iron-willed determination—but first and foremost by his trust in the Almighty. His praises were loudly proclaimed throughout all Ecuador, but his humble reply was, "Our gratitude should be addressed to God. It is He alone who has saved us....Therefore to God alone be love, honor, praise and glory, forever and ever. Amen."[21]

During his interim presidency, he outlined his expectations for the new constitution. He had two objectives: that the constitution would reflect the religious faith of the citizens, and that it would mandate the full powers needed to suppress and check the continued assaults of the revolution. He had no moral qualms about proposing strong executive powers for the government, since he was committed and determined to fulfill his oath of refusing to sit for the presidential elections once his interim term was completed.

The radicals, however, wary of the scope of the new constitution, once more plotted a violent takeover of the country. The revolt again centered in Guayaquil, but this time the loyalists were able to crush the insurgents without relying on Moreno's direct involvement. Nevertheless, this latest uprising convinced the populace and the deputies that he must renounce his oath and stand for election, since all their hopes for maintaining the stability of the nation were centered upon his leadership.

THE SECOND TERM: 1869-1875

Moreno resigned his post of Acting President in May of 1869, but when the electoral convention met in July they unanimously (less one dissenter) chose him as president for the coming term—which had been changed from four to six years under the new constitution. Moreno persisted in refusing the honor, while the deputies continued to insist that he was indispensable for the future of Ecuador. Finally they officially summoned him to be sworn in, and the reluctant hero had no other recourse but to obey.

He took the formal oath of office at the Cathedral in Quito, solemnly promising to fulfill his duties as president by observing the constitution and laws, and to profess and preserve the Catholic religion. Then, in reply to the dignitary who delivered the congratulatory speech, Moreno underscored the seriousness of his commitment to the oath of office: "Happy shall I be if I have to seal it with my blood, in defense of religion and my country."[22]

The new constitution, whose preparation he directed and inspired, was met with bitter rage by his enemies. They labeled it the "Black Charter," and the "Charter of Slavery to the Vatican."[23] This extreme reaction was likely sparked by a clause stating that only Roman Catholics would be eligible to hold public office or become members of the Chamber of Deputies.

In drafting the constitution, he was guided by the Syllabus of Errors, issued by Pope Pius IX only a few years before, in 1864. Moreno is reputed to have said that if the Syllabus remained a dead letter, society would be at an end. His biographer, Berthe, wrote that the new constitution of Ecuador "was in exact conformity to the principles of the Syllabus."[24]

For instance, nothing could be further removed from Moreno's vision of Church-State relations than the following propositions, all condemned by the Syllabus: "The teaching of the Catholic Church is hostile to the well-being and interests of Society" (No. 40); "The Church ought to be separated from the State, and the State from the Church" (No. 55); and "Moral laws do not stand in need of the divine sanction, and it is not at all necessary that human laws should be made conformable to the laws of nature and receive their power of binding from God (No. 56).[25] Moreno understood how important it was for the Church to formally denounce the errors condemned by the Syllabus, a Papal document that can never be superseded.

Backed by the new constitution, Moreno was ready to begin fulfilling in earnest his plans for a new Ecuador–but the enemy made one last futile attempt to stop him. Realizing that the country had now grown intolerant of the endless attempts at coups and revolutions, the leftists turned to their only alternative–assassination! The plot might have succeeded but for the remorse of one of the ringleaders, who revealed the details of the nefarious scheme to Moreno himself. The vile attempt was thwarted with the arrest of the would-be murderers.

A planned takeover of a major city, Cuenca, that was to occur in conjunction with the assassination, also met with failure. Unfortunately, the rebels were able to severely wound the Governor of the area, who barely escaped death. At their trial, the Cuenca insurgents were met with harsh sentences of either death or imprisonment with hard labor. When certain influential women citizens tried to intercede for the criminals, Moreno angrily replied that they should rather be concerned with the life-threatening condition in which the wounded governor lay. He pungently added, "When people remain deaf to the cries of the victims, they lose the right to plead for clemency in favor of assassins."[26]

By suppressing this last gasp of the revolution, the Moreno administration remained relatively unimpeded as it embarked on an amazing six years of effort, in which the entire nation of Ecuador was completely transformed. If a man is to be judged by his works, the accomplishments that Moreno attained during his second term as president were a resounding testimony to his greatness.

His overriding concern was to ensure that morality, security, and justice prevailed everywhere. To this end he undertook the reform of the clergy, the military, and the legal system.

The Apostolic Delegate that had been appointed in accordance with the Concordat had proved to lack the firmness necessary to correct the prevailing waywardness and laxity of the clergy. As a consequence, Moreno asked for and received a new delegate from Pope Pius IX. Ecclesiastical tribunals were resumed under stricter procedures, and provincial councils were held. The president also invited a great number of religious from overseas to populate the monasteries of Ecuador in order to impose greater discipline on those establishments. Many of the radicals living in neighboring countries issued broadsides protesting such religious "slavery." To these Moreno eloquently responded, "As to the impious pamphlets put out by the Freemasons of Columbia, I take as little account of them as of the pestilential miasmas of their distant marshes."[27]

On the national security front, he felt that only a small standing army was needed. However, he wanted a large body of fully trained reserves to be available in times of danger. To this end, he created a National Guard which periodically held military exercises for most of the able bodied men during the year. He also reformed a corrupt system of recruiting, eliminating the illegal "ransom" payments made to dishonest officials in order to avoid conscription. He did this by clearly defining the criteria for exemption from military service.

Creation of a cadet school for the training of career army officers was next. The most promising and intelligent of these men were sent to Europe, especially Prussia, to study the latest military strategies. This was not empty posturing, since Moreno spared no expense in procuring the newest and most efficient weaponry for his troops. In this way, the nation had at its disposal a small but very powerful army. This disciplined and well-equipped force was capable of standing up to any threat from tiny Ecuador's much larger neighbors.

Nor did he overlook the spiritual formation of his soldiers. Chaplains were appointed to every regiment, providing the sacraments, religious instruction, and even holding annual retreats. Instead of spending their free time in debauchery, many of the men began to lead pious lives and were inspired to improve themselves by attending night school.

On the legal front, he undertook a complete revision of the penal code, targeting "drunkards, debauchees, and disturbers of the public peace."[28] Homes were opened for the treatment and rehabilitation of alcoholics. Those who persisted in public intoxication or involvement in prostitution were either imprisoned or exiled. The new constitution empowered the government to weed out judges and magistrates who were dishonest or incompetent, allowing their replacement by men of upright conduct. Penalties were inflicted on unscrupulous lawyers who took advantage of the trust of their clients.

As significant as these accomplishments were, they are eclipsed by the magnificent advances instituted by the president in all areas of education. In order to implement his 1871 Education Bill, which mandated compulsory education of boys from the age of eight, he sought help from the teaching congregations of Europe. Soon the Christian Brothers, Sacred Heart Nuns, Sisters of Charity, and other orders arrived and were installed as teachers in the major cities. To provide qualified instructors for the outlying regions, he created a Normal College under the direction of the Christian Brothers to train lay teachers. As a result, enrollment in the primary schools soared within a few years from 8,000 to 32,000 boys in over 500 such schools. Unfortunately, traveling to school was considered too dangerous or inappropriate for girls. Undaunted, Moreno asked the Sacred Heart Nuns to open schools in their convents for female boarders and day students, for which parents were very grateful.

Nor were the native Indians neglected, with special schools established for their education. Schools were also founded for the children of soldiers and prisoners. In addition to all this, a vocational institute for boys was opened in order to teach useful trades such as carpentry and mechanics. It was staffed by Brothers of religious from New York. A similar program was inaugurated for girls from poor families, run by the Sisters of Providence from Belgium. In all cases, the teachers, whether lay Christians or religious, instilled piety as well as formal knowledge in their charges.

In order to correct the deficiencies in secondary and higher education, Moreno sought the assistance of the Jesuits. Colleges and academies were opened in Quito and throughout the country. Moreno also re-opened the University of Quito, which he had previously suppressed because it had become a hotbed of vice and "detestable doctrine." Thoroughly Catholic lay professors were assigned there, and a large number of German Jesuit Fathers were also recruited.

For the formation of engineers and technicians, a Polytechnic School was organized, adjacent to the university. The University of Quito also gave birth to a Faculty of Medicine, with professors of surgery and anatomy obtained from Montpellier, France. Overlooking nothing, Moreno commissioned a 300-bed hospital to be operated in conjunction with the medical school. All of these institutions needed equipment, and Moreno insisted on sending for the latest and best instruments and machines from overseas.

This was not all. He founded a School of Fine Arts, importing professors from Italy to teach sculpture and painting, and had the best students sent to Rome to complete their studies. He also inaugurated the Conservatory of Music, whose students provided free weekly concerts of both sacred and classical compositions.

The crowning achievement of his education reform was the building of the first South American astronomical observatory. He sought to take advantage of the clear mountain air and equatorial location of Quito. The telescope, at the time one of the three most advanced in the world, was crafted in Germany. The observatory is still functioning today with much of its original apparatus, and remains a popular tourist attraction.

Thus, in Moreno's second term as president, from 1869 to 1875, the culture of Ecuador was transformed from a state of mediocrity and neglect to one of excellence in all areas–education, science, medicine, technology, music and the arts. Everything was accomplished in accordance with Christian ethics, by employing only the best Catholic-educated instructors and professors. All in all, it was a magnificent testimony to the fecundity of Catholic civilization.

The Social Program

Moreno's program for the flowering of Ecuador was not lacking in social works of charity. He saw to the opening of two orphanages in Quito, staffed by religious sisters, with similar institutions soon budding in the other major cities. His concern for the moral standards of the nation led him to establish a "house of refuge for girls who had been led astray," also placed in the care of women religious.

He enjoyed striking success in the reform of the prison system, which was placed under the wise direction of a priest and an administrator, who transformed the jailhouses into veritable workshops and schools. Moreno himself made an annual examination not only of the system, but also of the progress of the prisoners in the skills they were learning.

He also succeeded in bringing an end to the plague of well-organized bandits that prowled the countryside. He realized that the most efficient way to end the brigandage was to strike at its head. Thus, he ordered an all out search for their leader, who was soon brought before him in shackles. Instead of being severely punished, the malefactor was surprised by an offer of clemency. The president would give the outlaw a chance to amend his life if he would consent to daily tutelage under a priest. The grateful man's turnaround was so complete that Moreno soon appointed him chief of police, with the specific mandate to convince his former colleagues in crime to voluntarily turn themselves over to the authorities. This they in fact did, trusting in Moreno's reputation for preferring rehabilitation over retribution. In this way he cleverly eliminated the scourge of the bandits. In fact, his policies for the treatment of criminals and prisoners were so effective that a new prison which he had ordered to be built in the capital ended up practically vacant. Indeed, by his last year in office in 1875, there were only fifty people still incarcerated in the prison system!

In the arena of public health, he began daily visits to the hospitals to evaluate their procedures and meet with patients. Finding that the lay nurses were undependable, he had all of the hospitals replace them with Sisters of Charity. He paid a special visit to the leper hospital and unexpectedly sat down with them to share their meal. Finding that their diet was inadequate, he ordered the necessary changes to be made.

The president was charitable not only with the financial resources of the State, but also with his personal income. Initially, he only accepted half of his salary, since the nation itself was so poor, and he donated the other half to various worthwhile causes. As the nation's finances improved, he accepted his full salary, but secretly used the whole of his official income to help those in need, especially the spouses and families of the revolutionaries that he had ordered into exile. Only after his death, when an official accounting of his papers was made, was the vast scope of his generosity revealed.

Garcia Moreno's missionary outreach to the 200,000 native South American Indians residing in the Amazon basin began during his first term. At that time there remained only the ruins of the old Jesuit missions that had been built in the Oriente during Spanish colonial rule one hundred years before. But the Jesuits had been driven out and kept out by the radicals during the periods of anti-clerical rule. In 1862, Moreno recalled them, and their missions were re-established. Near the start of his second term, in 1870, he placed these missions on a surer footing by creating schools that taught religion, the Spanish language, and basic subjects. He empowered local authorities to maintain order and protect the missionaries.

Although the rest of Ecuador was almost completely Catholic, there were serious priest shortages in many remote areas of the mountains and along the coast. He commissioned two groups of French Redemptorists to give retreats and missions, primarily in the isolated hamlets. These sessions usually lasted two weeks, with the enthusiastic faithful often traveling great distances to attend. The extremely popular events concluded with all those in attendance consecrating themselves and their families to the protection of the Blessed Virgin. The Redemptorists also made visits to the larger towns and cities. During their retreat in Quito, Moreno himself led a public procession, holding aloft the Crucifix, in the company of his deputies and ministers. Afterwards, he wrote to a friend, "God has blessed us; and the country is visibly improving....One would really imagine that God is bearing us up with His hand, like a tender father with his child when he tries to walk the first few steps."[29]

Consecration of the Nation to the Sacred Heart of Jesus

The Kings of France had ignored Our Lord's request, revealed in 1689 to St. Margaret Mary, to have their nation formally consecrated to His Sacred Heart. A desperate King Louis XVI, prior to his beheading by the Revolution in 1792, apparently privately consecrated the nation while he was in prison. Our Lord was to wait until 1873, when humble Ecuador became the first country to be publicly consecrated to His Sacred Heart by both the secular government and the Church. The accomplishment of this twofold consecration is attributable to Gabriel Garcia Moreno, and this act alone renders him worthy to stand among the greatest Catholic statesmen.

Jesuit Father Manuel Proano had earlier written to the President, suggesting the idea of the Consecration. Moreno's initial reply was that he did not feel that Ecuador was a worthy offering to the Sacred Heart of Jesus. He was not yet satisfied with the moral progress of the citizens. Characterizing the Heart of Jesus as the Throne of Wisdom, he wrote back to Fr. Proano questioning whether Ecuadorians were truly submissive to the Divine Teachings. Do justice and harmony reign in the nation? Is there true religious fervor? Has the domestic hearth been sanctified?[30] He informed Fr. Proano that when the people had been purified by the sending out of more "saintly missionaries, tireless apostles," he would then raise a church to the Sacred Heart.

Fr. Proano replied in turn that the Consecration would be an act of reparation for the conflicts and failings of the nation. Wisely, Moreno then decided to consult with the church hierarchy and with citizens who were fervent Catholics. The concept was favorably received, and Moreno gave it his support. Subsequently, the bishops attending the Third Quito Provincial Council performed the Consecration in the name of the Church on August 31, 1873. In the fall the Legislature voted in favor (with only one dissenter), decreeing an annual civic holiday to be celebrated with all solemnity. Then, on October 18, Moreno ratified, in the name of the State, the decree declaring the Most Sacred Heart of Jesus as the Patron and Protector of Ecuador.

On October 18 of the next year, the first anniversary of the Consecration was celebrated in every church of the nation. Garcia Moreno attended the ceremonies in the Cathedral of Quito, with the leading government and military officials in attendance. The Archbishop renewed the Consecration on behalf of the Church, and Moreno followed by proclaiming it on behalf of the State.

Moreno was never to witness another anniversary of the Consecration. His enemies had become enraged by this act of Christian piety. He was warned that the lodges in Germany had given orders to those in America to utterly overthrow the government of Ecuador. The Grand Council of the Order had condemned him to death.[31] In order to manipulate public opinion, journals in Europe and America began an organized campaign of denunciation of the President.

Almost as noteworthy as the Consecration was Ecuador's distinction of being the only nation in the world to officially protest Garibaldi's occupation of Rome and seizure of the Papal territories in order to create a unified Italy. In September of 1870, Pope Pius IX became "the prisoner of the Vatican" after the Papal city fell to the revolutionaries. Garcia Moreno addressed an official protest to the government of King Victor Emmanuel on behalf of Ecuador. He accused Italy of a "hateful and sacrilegious assault" in depriving the Holy Father of his temporal domains and incomes, thereby impeding the liberty of the Church to fulfill its Divine Mission.

Disappointed that the countries of the Old World made no protest against the injustice, Moreno appealed to the governments of the American continent to stand with Ecuador, but none dared follow suit. Thus small, insignificant Ecuador stood alone in her public indictment of the theft of the Papal States and properties. Although their governments were cowardly, the people of Europe stood in amazement and grateful admiration at Ecuador's defense of the Church. Pope Pius is said to have exclaimed, "Ah, if he was a powerful king the Pope would have someone to rely on in this world!"[32] In thanksgiving, the Holy Father heaped congratulations and honor upon Moreno, making him a Knight of the First Class of the Order of Pius IX.[33]

But the President was not content with merely verbally supporting the Pope. He proposed that Congress contribute some part of its own meager resources to financially support the Vatican, now deprived of a large part of its revenues. In 1873, the enthusiastic government officials unanimously voted to present the Holy Father with a national gift of 10,000 piastres–a relatively large sum, equivalent to over six million 2006 U.S. dollars.[34]

During these events, an exchange of letters took place between the Pope and the President. In praising the accomplishments of Moreno, the Holy Father went so far as to attribute his exceptional success to "a very special Divine intervention."[35] Moreno wrote back that Ecuador truly owed everything to God, refusing to attribute any merit to himself. He revealed the strength of his Catholic Faith by adding, "May God enlighten me, direct me in all things, and grant me the grace to die for the defense of the Faith and of Holy Church."[36] Shortly after his re-election to another six-year term in May of 1875, God saw fit to grant this grace.

His 1875 electoral victory was essentially unanimous since the opposition candidate withdrew, realizing it would be futile to run against Moreno. The electors, 23,000 in number, had no hesitation in voting for the man they hailed as the "saviour of the country." By contrast, the revolution, faced with the prospect of six more years of Catholic rule, determined that this was the moment to execute the decree for his assassination.

That summer the conspirators seemed everywhere. Amid a flood of warnings, his supporters beseeched the president to take immediate measures to protect himself. But Moreno refused to augment his guard or curtail his activities, choosing to commit his destiny to the Most High. He had become convinced that there was little that could be done to avoid the web of evil closing in on him. His reaction to the threats was to fortify himself with prayer and trust in God, steeling himself to accept what he saw as his inevitable martyrdom.

In July of 1875, he wrote his last letter to Pope Pius IX, informing him of his re-election and asking the Holy Father's apostolic blessing for the strength and light to remain faithful to God and the Church. He explained the reasons for the urgent need for divine protection for himself and for Ecuador, explaining "that the lodges of our neighboring countries, instigated by those of Germany, vomit against me all kinds of atrocious insults and horrible slander...."[37] Yet, Moreno accepted such detraction with Christ-like resignation, writing that it was his good fortune to suffer slander and scorn for the cause of the Redeemer. In words befitting the saint that he was, he continued: "And what joy, so immense for me...to spill my blood for Him, being God, who wanted to spill His own on the Cross for us!"[38]

Three weeks later, August 6th arrived. It was the first Friday of the month and the Feast of the Transfiguration. Early that morning at 6:00 o'clock, he attended Mass and received Holy Communion at the Dominican church near his home and offices in Quito. Perhaps sensing it was to be his Viaticum, he remained at the church in prayer and thanksgiving until 8:00 o'clock. The assassins would have struck as he left the church, but they were fearful of the large number of potential witnesses present.

Moreno returned home to work on the major address he was to deliver in a few days before the National Congress. After lunch he began walking to the Presidential Palace along with only one aide-de-camp. He stopped first at the Cathedral to spend some time in prayer before the Blessed Sacrament, which was exposed during the daytime hours. Small groups of conspirators had been hanging about the central Plaza throughout the day. One of their leaders, Faustino Lemos Rayo, became concerned that the long minutes the president was spending in adoration would upset the timing of their plans.

Rayo arranged to have a messenger enter the Cathedral and tell the president that his presence was needed for some important business. Upon hearing this, Moreno departed the Cathedral and made for the Presidential Palace, a short distance away. As he climbed the steps to the entrance, Rayo approached and whipped out a huge machete from underneath his cloak. He struck the president on the shoulder and head, while crying out "Die, Tyrant!"[39]

Other assassins emerged from behind columns and commenced firing revolvers at the staggering and bleeding victim. There were shouts of "Die, you Jesuit!" The dying Moreno was able to utter in return, "God does not die!" Too late, a crowd of citizens and officials chased the murderers away, and an army sergeant shot and killed Rayo in the middle of the Plaza. Moreno, still breathing, was carried into the Cathedral and placed at the foot of Our Lady of Sorrows. A surgeon arrived but could do nothing in the face of the half-dozen bullet wounds and innumerable machete blows. A priest was able to administer Extreme Unction to Moreno, who expired after indicating that he forgave his killers.

He had been wearing two scapulars, one of the Passion and the other of the Sacred Heart. A relic of the True Cross was found attached to his Rosary along with a medal bearing an image of Pope Pius IX. The notes containing his agenda for the day were found in his pocket. On the last page he had composed this short and profound prayer, which is nothing less than a compendium of the spiritual life: "My Saviour, Jesus Christ, give me greater love for Thee and profound humility, and teach me what I should do this day for Thy greater glory and service."[40]

NOTES

1. Fr. Manuel Sousa Pereira, *The Admirable Life of Mother Mariana*, tr. Marian T. Horvat, Ph.D. (Los Angeles: Tradition in Action, Inc., 1999), pp. 141-142.
2. George I. Blanksten, *Ecuador: Constitutions and Caudillos* (New York: Russell & Russell, Inc., 1964), p. 9.
3. Honorable Mrs. Maxwell-Scott, *Gabriel Garcia Moreno, Regenerator of Ecuador* (London: R. & T. Washbourne, Ltd., 1914), p. 40. [Reissued by the Apostolate of Our Lady of Good Success, 2004.]
4. *Ibid.*, p. 3.
5. Rev. Augustine Berthe, *Garcia Moreno, President of Ecuador* (London: Burns and Oates, Ltd., 1889), p. 112. [Reissued by Paul M. Kimball, Booksurge, LLC, 2006.]
6. *Ibid.*, pp. 131-134.
7. *Ibid.*, pp. 140-149.
8. *Ibid.*, pp. 274-278.
9. *The Catholic Encyclopedia* (1908), s.v. "Concordat," accessed online at www.newadvent.org.
10. Berthe, *President of Ecuador*, p. 164.
11. *Ibid.*, p. vi.
12. *Ibid.*, p. 170.
13. *Ibid.*, p. 167.
14. *Ibid.*, p. 182.
15. *Ibid.*, p. 184.
16. *Ibid.*, p. 208.
17. *Ibid.*, p. 211.
18. *Ibid.*, p. 230.
19. *Ibid.*
20. *Ibid.*, p. 234.
21. *Ibid.*, p. 236.
22. *Ibid.*, p. 243.
23. Blanksten, *Ecuador*, p. 12.
24. Berthe, *President of Ecuador*, p. 245.
25. Anthony J. Mioni, Jr., ed., *The Popes Against Modern Errors* (Rockford, Illinois: TAN Books & Publishers, 1999), pp. 33-36.
26. Berthe, *President of Ecuador*, p. 251.
27. *Ibid.*, p. 253.
28. *Ibid.*, p. 256.
29. *Ibid.*, p. 273.
30. Francisco Salazar Alvarado, *Encounter with History: Garcia Moreno, Catholic Leader of Latin America* (Oconomowoc, Wisconsin: Apostolate of Our Lady of Good Success, 2006), p. 95.

[31] Maxwell-Scott, *Regenerator of Ecuador,* p. 152.
[32] *Ibid.,* p. 130.
[33] Berthe, *President of Ecuador,* p. 308.
[34] *Ibid.,* p. 309, n. 1.
[35] Maxwell-Scott, *Regenerator of Ecuador,* p. 131.
[36] *Ibid.,* p. 133.
[37] Alvarado, *Encounter with History,* p. 161.
[38] *Ibid.*
[39] *Ibid.,* p. 41.
[40] Berthe, *President of Ecuador,* p. 325.

Bibliography

Alvarado, Francisco Salazar. *Encounter with History: Garcia Moreno, Catholic Leader of Latin America.* Oconomowoc, Wisconsin: Apostolate of Our Lady of Good Success, 2006.

Berthe, Rev. Fr. Augustine. *Garcia Moreno, President of Ecuador.* London: Burns and Oates, Ltd., 1889. [Reissued by Paul M. Kimball, Booksurge, LLC, 2006.]

Blanksten, George I. *Ecuador: Constitutions and Caudillos.* New York: Russell & Russell, Inc., 1964.

Maxwell-Scott, Honorable Mrs. *Gabriel Garcia Moreno, Regenerator of Ecuador.* London: R. & T. Washbourne, Ltd., 1914. [Reissued by the Apostolate of Our Lady of Good Success, Oconomowoc, Wisconsin, 2004.]

Mioni, Anthony J. Jr., Editor. *The Popes Against Modern Errors.* Rockford, Illinois: TAN Books and Publishers, 1999.

Pereira, Fr. Manual Sousa. *The Admirable Life of Mother Mariana,* translated by Marian T. Horvat, Ph.D. Los Angeles: Tradition in Action, Inc., 1999.